Sunday Summer
Someone to Love Me...

Anne Gaynelle Johnson

Hov
PUBLISHING

Sunday Summer
Someone to Love Me...

HOV Publishing a division of HOV, LLC.
www.hovpub.com
hopeofvision@gmail.com

Cover Design: HOV Design Solutions
Editor: Caroline Barnhill for Oak & State, LLC.

Write the Author Anne Gaynelle Johnson at:
christworkshop@yahoo.com

For more information about special discounts for bulk purchases, please contact: christworkshop@yahoo.com.

ISBN: 978-1-942871-73-6
eBook ISBN: 978-1-942871-74-3

Library of Congress Control Number:

10   9   8   7   6   5   4   3   2   1

Printed in the United States of America

DEDICATION

I pray you enjoy this two-part book written with you all in mind.

I dedicate this book to some of my special young ladies, including my granddaughters T'nya, Shayleen, Tenesha, Kennadia, Tae'lor, Moriah, Tenaye, Taylor, and Heather; some precious young women I've met through T'nya: Deva, Pilar, Kyleen, Tia, Lenise, Amani; my Sister Robbieann Davis' granddaughters: Cheyenne, Rachel and Taylor; my spiritual daughter Evangelist Sheria Stalling' daughters: Maya and Charlee; Evangelist Nanette Elmore's daughter Rachel; my goddaughters: Sahara, Traci, Tiffany,

Shauntay, Crystal and Felicia; Bessie Taylor's granddaughter Diamond (I call her a diamond in the rough because she is a hardworking young woman); Frances Castro's granddaughter Felicia Castro who is a very courageous, strong, loving, caring young woman; Walika Mainor; Raven Butler (Raven, I'm so proud of you for graduating from college with your degree); my grandnieces: Sapoo, Keisha, Meek-Meek, Lil Momma, LaToy, Danielle (Nikki); and to all the young women reading this book. I also would like to dedicate this book to some young women in my church who inspire me with their desire to please God: sister Sofia Cumberbatch who is in college, raising a daughter, and who has grown to be a strong, praying woman of

iv

God right before my eyes; Moet Bolden, another college graduate who has weathered the storms of life and survived; Kima Reid; Crystal Cruz; Angelia Reid, who is married with three beautiful children and who went back to college and earned her degree; aspiring missionary Marcy Smith, who always encouraged me in so many ways; and to two special young women who have a special place in my heart: to sister Melanie Jackson and her sister Christina Johnson, and to Dionna Marshburn and her daughter Nia. These women allowed me to help train them in their singing and it proved to be productive as they grew in womanhood. I want all of you to know that God has everything you will ever need. All you have to do is keep living holy lives and stay sweetly saved – and nothing will be impossible to you. Put God first in all that you do and always pray before you accept, act or do anything, I pray that as you read this book, you too will be inspired to encourage a younger woman following in your footsteps to sing, pray and find the talent hidden within her to use it for God's glory. Plant a seed of this book in some young girl's life. Finally, thank you to my dear friend, prayer sister and supporter in ministry for years, Elder Brenda Little, and to her dear daughters Pam and Octavia.

You are now on your way to the best part, the conclusion of the whole matter.

TABLE OF CONTENTS

PREFACE

This book is fictional and is intended to encourage our young ladies to wait on God and be of good courage. He will strengthen your hearts. Get your education and set your goals high in life, for God has great things for you. Don't be in a hurry to find love. Believe me, it will find you in time and it will be perfect and right. Train up your children to always obey you and follow after Jesus Christ. When Mr. Right comes along, he will be prepared for only you. Don't be swayed into temporary relationships and situations that leave you heartbroken and depressed because you were so desperate for love. Love is patient and love is kind (I Corinthians 13:4).

Don't allow any man to abuse you and keep you quiet. When you see red flags in your relationships, run for your life. You are strong, beautiful, successful, determined and destined to reign. You are a woman of every race, creed and color. Don't let anyone define you by their convictions; you are justified by faith and God has given you every promise in the Holy Bible. You can do all things through Christ who strengthens you. God's strength is made perfect when you feel weak. Lean on Him, trust Him, depend on Him, and communicate with Him through prayer daily – He will talk back to you, instruct you, provide for you, and orchestrate all things.

Don't let your heart give in to lies and deceit. Deception has no color. God has got you, so don't listen to fake friends who lure you into abusive, merely sexual relationships. A good man's steps are ordered by the Lord – and a good guy is what He has for each of you. I wish someone had written a book telling me this. As a teenager, I used to read romance books – though the stories were so intriguing, some were sad and hurtful. A lot of pain and suffering could be avoided if someone shared with us. In these days, many have shut up their bowels of compassion. But not me. God has given me this book series just for you. Enjoy, girls. You are on your way to greater things in Christ Jesus. You are blessed. *~With Love, Sister Anne*

INTRODUCTION

I was standing in the kitchen cooking as I remembered I had spoken to my son "Doobie" and asked, "Who is the baby you are with on Facebook?," and he answered, "That's *Summer*, Keisha's baby girl." I said that she is beautiful and that her name sounds like a book title. Keisha is my great niece, so Summer is my great-great niece. Doobie said, "Ma, you going to write a book about her?" I simply said no, but that I would use her name. So, I sat down at the computer and thought about what a good name to title this book would be... and it came to my thoughts: *Sunday Summer*. My great-great niece looks like a ray of sun with her cute smile. I said, "That's what I'll call it, but I'm going to write it as a two-part book. Sunday Summer being born and her finding happiness at the end to heal the hurt she has encountered in life through falling in love."

So here I go, putting on my thinking cap and looking to God to word my fingers. The first people I thought about were the young women of today. I see their struggle with children and when talking with many of them, I always hear about this boy or that boy who they are in love with. And sometimes I hear a sad story about how one of these boys went off with another girl and lied to her. And being a rape victim myself, I would include it in my writings. So, I said to myself, "Lord, young women need

encouragement and that's where I come in."
I've experienced a lot in life: I had three
children out of wedlock, broke off an
engagement when I realized I didn't love the
man, and remained single. Life's choices are
given to us by our Creator, God, who freely
gives to each of us a measure of faith. I can
say that I had one true love in life. I
wouldn't marry him and I let go of a "good
guy" at the age of eighteen – in case
someone reading this book thinks they know
who I'm talking about. It was in Richmond,
Virginia and we had a loving relationship. I
can, and will always, say he is one of the
most exceptional men I've met in my life.
So girls, when you see him coming, don't
pass him up for the "bad boy" who comes as
a wolf in sheep's clothing looking like he

was born with a silver spoon in his mouth and talking ever so smooth and cool. To be honest, the spoon is tarnished. I want to stir up your pure minds so you can find happiness in life, security and true love. Enjoy reading *Sunday Summer*. This is a fictional story. Thanks to my own daughters, Linda and Hope. You are my encouragement. I thank God for you.

Love, Evangelist Anne

CHAPTER 1

Move-In-Day-Surprise!

It's a bright sunny day in May. Clarice and Clark Summer have just moved into their new home that they've been saving money for five years to buy. It's a ranch-style home with three bedrooms and two and a half baths. It also has a full basement, a den for Clark's business, a formal dining room, a living room and a large kitchen with an island – with a family room in sight. They also have a deck built on the back with a large backyard. They are excited – it's their first house.

Clarice and Clark plan to have three children. They desire a boy first and then two girls, but God has other plans for them when it comes to which gender will come first. Clarice has just walked into the den and she is smiling at Clark.

"What's wrong?" Clark asks. "What are you smiling about, baby?"

Clarice holds up the pregnancy test strip. "We're pregnant, Clark."

"Oh, thank God for answering our prayers," Clark says, jumping for joy. "A new house…and our family has started to grow already. God is always on time. Does that test say it's a boy?"

"No, silly," says Clarice, "it's just telling us to expect a bundle of joy."

2

Clark jumps up and tenderly kisses Clarice. 'I love you, Mrs. Summer. You are my special lady. And I don't want you standing on your feet so much," he says as he sits down.

Hitting him on the shoulder, Clarice laughs, "I'm not an invalid, I'm pregnant. I will make an appointment with Doctor Taye tomorrow. Okay?"

Clark and Clarice are beaming with joy. Clark calls his parents. "Mom, we're pregnant. You're going to be a grandma! Tell dad when he gets home."

"Oh son, I'm so elated," Mrs. Geraldine says. "I can't wait until Jorge gets home so I can tell him the good news."

Clarice calls her mom. "Mrs. Dancie, you are going to be a grandmother," she says.

"Oh dad, please tell him when he comes from church. We are so excited – you are going to be a babysitter soon."

"I can go for that, darling," Mrs. Dancie says, smiling.

Oh, what a happy day at 1243 Loving Hearts Lane. There is so much joy and happiness being shared. Truly, God has favored Clarice and Clark Summer.

"What will we name the baby?" Clarice asks Clark. "If it's a boy, of course Clark, Jr., but if it's a girl, we will name her Sunday. I've always loved that name."

"Whatever you say, darling," Clark replies, "is what the baby's name will be. I love you so much, my lady love."

"Oh Clark, I love you, too. You make me so happy, honey."

"Well, what about dinner?" Clark asks. "The baby has to eat healthy, you know… and get plenty of water."

"I'm pregnant…I thank God. Oh God, thank You so much."

"Should we throw a pregnant party and invite everyone to celebrate with us, honey?"

"No Clark, we'll wait for the baby shower. Honey, you are really excited about our baby!" Clarice says. "I'm glad you are my husband,"

"And I'm glad you are my wife, Clarice," says Clark, kissing her.

"How about the house warming and baby shower together?"

"That would be a plus," Clark says. "Let's start planning now. We'll call our parents to help out with the plans."

"Clark, I'm so excited about our new life," Clarice says. "Whatever God is doing, let's thank Him for our blessings."

They begin to pray thankful prayers.

CHAPTER 2

A Visit to Doctor Taye's – Boy or Girl?

Dr. Taye walks out of her office and sees two happy, smiling faces looking at her. "Clarice and Clark Summer, please come into my office. How are the two of you today? I heard the excitement in your voices over the phone and it's written all over your faces. Congratulations on your pregnancy."

"Thank you, Dr. Taye," Clarice says. "Clark and I are excited to know what gender our baby is."

"Okay, you two excitable parents, then we will take a sonogram. Clarice, get undressed, put on a gown and my nurse will be in to prepare you for the procedure. Okay?

"Clark, that's a mighty big smile on your face. That's wonderful for an expectant dad. You and Clarice will find out what gender your bundle of joy is soon – but first, I need to ask you a couple of questions. Do twins run in your family?"

"No," says Clarice, "not in mine."

"Not that I know of," Clark says. "Do you think it could be…"

"No," Clark and Clarice say at once."

"Okay," Dr. Taye says. "It's just a question I ask expectant parents. If so, we want to make sure we check everything thoroughly, that's all. Let me see if Kathy has the room ready.

" Kathy, is the room ready?" Dr. Taye asks on the intercom.

"Yes, they can come in now," Kathy replies.

"Well, you two, let's get this ball to rolling," Dr. Taye says. "Come with me."

Dr. Taye leads them into the exam room. "Okay mom, lay on the table. Clarice, I need you to be still. This is a little cold, but it is instant. Now look at the screen. See the baby's feet."

"Oh my!" Clark says with tears in his eyes. "It's our first baby. Hey Dr. Taye, do I see a girl part?"

"Yes, you do, you are having a baby girl," Dr. Taye says. "See, Clarice?"

"Oh yes, I do," Clarice says.

"It seems you are farther along than you thought," Dr. Taye says, measuring her stomach. "Yes, you are about twelve weeks pregnant. I'll send your prescription for prenatal vitamins over to the pharmacy. I'll see you in six weeks. Go ahead and get dressed, Clarice. The sonogram printout will be at the front desk. God bless you two."

"Dr. Taye," Clark says, "can I ask a simple question?"

"Sure, ask away."

"Well, I don't want to do any damage to my wife while she's pregnant and I just want to know…well, I feel a little embarrassed asking this."

Clarice interrupts. "Dr. Taye, how long can we be sexually active? Is there a point where it is dangerous to make love?

Clark doesn't want to do anything to hurt the baby or me."

"Well, you determine how long that happens. I mean, if you want to make love to your wife, you can. When she gets in her ninth month, you can see how it affects her – if she is having a painful time, then you'll know. But son, enjoy your wife. That's why you are married. God said marriage is honorable and the bed is undefiled. So that's your wife, enjoy each other. Now, after the baby is born, I would ask that you wait until her six-week checkup. She needs time to heal and purify her body again. Does that help you at all, Clark?"

Clark smiles. "Yes, Dr. Taye." He looks at Clarice. "Thanks honey for bringing that out for me. Well doc, we will be on our way home. We are going to start decorating for our little baby girl. No one knows right now, but God, how excited and happy I am about little Sunday coming into our lives!"

"Oh," says Dr. Taye, "you picked a name already!"

"Yes, Clarice and I picked her name. She will be the sunshine God gives us to brighten our lives. And her middle name is going to be Marie…after my great, great grandmother. She was a missionary and she loved children. As a matter of fact, she and my great-great-grandpa had 13 children of their own."

"Wow, you come from a large family and no twins?"

"Oh yes, they had two sets of twins. A set of boys and a set of girls. But we have one baby girl. Clarice, maybe our next children will be twins!"

"Clark, let's cross that bridge when we get to it," Clarice says. "Thank you for the visit, Dr. Taye. It was a pleasure."

"Clarice, get plenty of rest and drink water. And no sodas or spicy, greasy foods, okay? We want a healthy delivery. See you two in six weeks."

CHAPTER 3

How Time Flies

Clark walks into the kitchen. "Good evening honey, how is my beautiful queen? I thought maybe we could go out for dinner tonight so you don't have to stand on your feet so much preparing food."

"Honey, I'm a little famished," Clarice says. "I've been having little twanging pains. I called Dr. Taye and she said it's normal when the pregnancy gets closer to delivery date. Can we skip going out and order in? I'm not feeling too much on dining out tonight."

"Okay, whatever you want. Want to order some Boston Market rotisserie chicken and mashed potatoes and veggies?"

"Sounds like dinner to me, honey."

"Clarice, where did we put that number?"

"Look at the board in the kitchen. It should be right there. Listen, I'm going to lie down on the sofa...I feel a little tired and achy. Okay, baby?"

Clark kisses her ever so tender and says, "Whatever you want to do, baby. Do you want me to go down there and get it, or should I order it for delivery?"

"No Clark, they will deliver, and as a matter of fact, they are pretty fast. I want you here with me. Suppose the baby comes while you are at the store."

15

"Oh no, Clarice, I won't leave you baby. That's why I took this time off from work – so I could be home with you."

Clark goes into the kitchen and places the order. "Okay, baby cakes, I ordered and they said fifteen minutes. That's fast. Hey, you look a little tired. Here, lie down and I'll get you a blanket to put over your legs."

"Thanks Clark. Honey, I feel like I weigh 50 tons. But this little bundle of joy is going to be very welcome here." Clarice lays down, put her feet up and falls fast asleep.

The doorbell rings. "Coming!" Clark says. He answers the door. "Thank you for such prompt service. Here's a nice tip for you. Have a good evening."

Walking into the room, Clark says, "Clarice, dinner is served." He finds her fast asleep. "Wow, my baby is tired. I'll just wait till later to eat…think I'll just watch a little television while she sleeps."

"Hm, Hm, oh, oh," Clarice moans. She gets up from sofa and calls to Clark, "Where are you, Clark? I need you in here!"

Running into the room, Clark says, "Oh honey, you couldn't make it to the bathroom. I'll get the mop and bucket and clean it up."

"Clark, get back in here. Baby, my water just broke. Call Dr. Taye. Sunday is ready to come."

Clark runs to get his phone and calls Dr. Taye. "Hello," he says nervously. "Doc, the baby is coming. Clarice's water just broke."

"Get to the hospital right away," Dr. Taye says. "I'll be there waiting for you three."

"Okay, we're on our way, doc," Clark says. "Clarice, do you need me to call an ambulance or can you walk to the car with my help?"

"I can walk, Clark. Just help me please."

"Hold onto me, I got you, baby love."

Clark is careful with Clarice as he sees the contractions coming faster. "Hold on Clarice and Sunday, daddy's got you."

They arrive at the hospital safely, where Dr. Taye is waiting with the stretcher. "We're here, baby," Clark says, helping

Clarice onto the stretcher and wheeling her into the birthing room.

"Clark, put on this gown and wash your hands," Dr. Taye says. "You are going to see God at work and your wife deliver your baby girl."

Sunday is born.

As the baby cries, Dr. Taye hands her to Clarice. "Here is your beautiful, six pounds and five ounces baby girl: little Sunday Marie Summer. Congratulations. Clarice, I'm going to keep you for a couple of days. That's my way of treating my patients. Then you can go home and take Sunday to her new home."

As Clark cries and touches Sunday, he says, "She is so cute. I love you, Clarice."

"I love you too, Clark. Isn't she all that we thought she would be?"

"She is so perfect. Oh Sunday, mommy and daddy love you. You are our bundle of joy from God." He prays, "Thank you Lord for our blessing. We promise to love her and bring her up to know you always."

Dr. Taye walks in the room. "Clark, Clarice needs to get some sleep. So, you can sit in here with her and Sunday, okay? See you three in the morning." The phone rings. "Well, no sleep for the doctor! There's another delivery. Listen Clarice, get some rest. The nurse will be in soon with her formula – or will you be breastfeeding?"

"No Dr. Taye, we are giving her formula."

"Okay, fine, I already prescribed everything for Sunday Marie. Good night. I've got to go."

"Good night, Dr. Taye. Clark, honey, did the food delivery come?"

"As a matter of fact, it came quick while you were resting and I left it out on the stove. I need to go home and put it in the refrigerator. Listen, you rest and I'll be back in the morning."

"Okay, honey. She is resting so peacefully, isn't she? Clark, go home and get some sleep. I'm a little tired myself."

"Good night, Sunday Marie," Clark says, kissing Sunday. "Daddy will see you in the morning." He kisses Clarice. "Goodnight, sweetheart."

CHAPTER 4

Sunday at Sixteen

Sunday Marie has grown up to be quite a beautiful young lady. She has grown an interest in boys and spotted one she wants to talk to while at a college football game. His name is Avery Talik Howard. Sunday wrote him a letter stating that she is interested in him and he responded saying that he is interested in her, too. He saw her in the library near the school the other day and asked his friend to get her name and number.

The only thing is Avery is nineteen years old and a college student. That doesn't bother Sunday. She is accustomed to always getting what she wants – and she wants Avery. Sunday has a set of twin brothers, Clark, Jr. and Calvin. They are ten years old and they love their older sister; they look up to her. Sunday has stopped spending time with them and reading to them, instead giving all her interest to pursuing Avery.

One day, Mother Thomas from the church saw Sunday kissing Avery on the lips. She said to her, "Young lady, do your mother and father know you have a boyfriend?"

Sunday says that he is only a friend and explains that she was consoling him because his team lost the football game.

"Well, young lady, you need to be more careful how you carry yourself out here in public."

"Yes ma'am, Mother Thomas, I will. I'm sorry."

Mother Thomas goes off shopping.

"Wow, she sure has a grip on you, Sunday," Avery says.

"Listen Avery, I know we should not have been caught kissing in public. I pray she doesn't breathe it to my parents...I'll be on restriction and then I won't be able to see you, honey bug."

"Sunday, why don't you come to my apartment on Friday after school? We can spend some quality time together. Can you get away?"

"Well, I can always tell my parents that I have to study a paper with one of my friends," she says. "What are we going to do? You know I'm a virgin and I intend to stay that way until we get married."

"Wait a minute, Sunday, you are going a little too fast for me. Marriage? You are sixteen and still in school. I'm still in college. You have to get there, baby love."

"I know, Avery, but if we are going to act grown up, we must make plans. You said you love me. Do you?"

"Of course I do, baby, but let's not move too quickly. I'm planning on going away to medical school in two more years. And you won't be graduating for another year."

"Avery, I'll be seventeen years old in another month. And I'm graduating next June. Come on, we can make plans, can't we?"

"Sure we can, if you can prove to me that you're my girl."

"How Avery? You mean have sex with you? I can't do that. That would be breaking my promise that I made to God and to myself that I will wait until I'm married. You can respect that, can't you?"

"Okay, so we'll wait."

"Oh Avery, I do love you and trust you. I have to go. I promised Clark Jr. and Calvin that I would watch a movie with them tonight. And I don't think it is wise to come to your apartment. Something might happen and cause us problems. And I want to stay a virgin. I'm proud of being untouched and you should be too. Avery, have you ever done it with a girl?"

"No Sunday, I'm waiting for you. You are my one and only true love. Listen Sunday, I'm on my way to study hall. See you later."

"Okay, call me later?"

"Okay, if I finish studying early. See you, baby love."

Avery seems a little disappointed that he can't get Sunday to his house, but in fact, he lied to her – he's been seeing another girl named Angie and they seem pretty close sometimes. I hope that Sunday sticks to her promise to stay a clean young lady until marriage. But you know, and I know, that some guys are very convincing.

As Sunday walks into her house, she says, "Mom, dad, I'm home. Mom, you look a little upset, what's wrong?"

"Well, Sunday, Mother Thomas called and told me she saw you kissing some older boy on the lips. Honey, I told you always to be careful."

"Mom, I feel that she is nosy and should mind her own business. I am almost seventeen and I have a right to talk to boys."

"Not if they are older. That boy is in college. He will take advantage of you, Sunday. What are you thinking? You aren't ready to handle a man at your age, honey."

"Mom, I'm not having sex, if that's what's on your mind. I am in love with Avery – and he loves me."

"Wait a minute, young lady, you are not allowed to date at your age. We have not given you that permission, so you need to break it off with him. Do you understand?"

"Yes mom, I understand," Sunday says, crying. She runs out of the kitchen.

Clarice begins to pray, "Lord, please don't let Sunday be a fast girl. Let her realize that she has a lot to do in her life and that boys can wait. Please God, help us."

Sunday walks back into the kitchen. "Mom, I'll be seventeen in three weeks. Will I be allowed to date Avery then? I know he is nineteen, but he is special to me and he is kind and we love one another."

"Sunday, that is too soon to know that you are in love with someone. What about college and graduate school? How can you

29

be a medical surgeon if you start dating boys now and having sex? Because that's all they want from loose girls."

"Mom, I told you I'm not sexually active. I'm a virgin. And I don't carry myself like a loose girl."

"Yes, until he lures you into a tight spot and convinces you to prove your love to him."

"Is that what dad did to you, mom?"

Clarice slaps Sunday. "Young lady, you apologize to me right now."

"I'm sorry mom, but you hit me. Why?"

"Because you are being disrespectful."

"Well, say you are sorry you slapped me."

"I'm not apologizing to you, Sunday. And because you are trying to be too grown, go to your room. I'll call you when dinner is ready."

"Mom, I'm not hungry. I'm hurt and embarrassed that I have to tell the man I love that it's over."

"Well, it should have never started... then you wouldn't have had to tell him anything."

Sunday goes to her room. She hears a knock on her door. "Who is it?"

"Calvin and Clark, Jr. Are we watching the movie tonight like you promised, Sunday?" the twins ask.

"Open the door and come in, you two. I'm a little tired. Can we do this another time, you guys?"

"Okay, maybe the weekend, huh?

"Yeah, the weekend. Go do your homework. I need to read a book for school. Okay guys?"

"See you later, big sister."

Sunday immediately calls Avery. He doesn't answer. *Where is he,* she wonders. *Oh, in study hall. Avery is true to me,* she tells herself. *He would never lie to me. God, how can I break it off with my one true love? How can I let him go? Mom is going to make me hate her for this. If I lose Avery, my world will end.*

Is Sunday considering suicide? We need to find out.

The next morning, Sunday says, "Mom, I'm going to be late coming home. I

32

have study hall after school with Mr. Fisher. Mom, are you in there?"

"Yes," Clarice answers. "Make sure you come straight home from study hall. Don't make me start checking behind you, Sunday.

Sunday leaves, slamming the door.

I've got to go by the college to see Avery, Sunday thinks. *No, I know what. I'll stop by his apartment and break the bad news to him.* As she approaches Avery's apartment, she's upset. She knocks on the door. "Avery, are you in there? Answer the door."

"Just a moment," an unfamiliar voice call from inside. The door opens wide. "Hi, may I help you?"

"Well, yes," Sunday says, "I'm looking for Avery Howard. He's my boyfriend."

"Really! Well, he's in the shower. Would you like to leave him a message? Who are you, may I ask? I'm Angie, his fiancé. And you say you are his girlfriend? I don't think so."

Sunday pushes pass Angie and opens the bathroom door. "Well, Avery, what is going on?" she says, crying. "So, you have a fiancé? When was I supposed to find out?"

"Sunday, I was going to tell you, but you kept insisting that we were getting married…I know you are young and I didn't want to hurt you, baby."

"Baby? I'm not your baby. Angie is. Liar. My mom was right." As she walks out, she wipes her eyes and says, "Sorry Angie, my bad."

Sunday is so hurt by Avery. She returns home in tears. "Mom, mom, I need you now,"

Clarice rushes into the living room. "Baby, what's wrong?" she asks, hugging Sunday.

"Mom, he lied to me. I went to his house to tell him it's over and he had another woman there. She said she was his fiancé. How could he lie to me like that? I hate him. I don't want to live, mom. I don't want to live!"

Clarice grabs Sunday. "The Blood of Jesus, you stop talking that foolishness, okay? Listen to me. I rebuke that demonic spirit of suicide right now. And you went to his house, how could you, girl? You are looking for trouble. Sunday, you have two brothers who look up to you. This is not the end of the world. It's better that you found out now rather than later after giving yourself to him. Calm yourself, Sunday."

"Mom, I was so angry with you for slapping me and telling me to end our relationship that I was going to his house to sleep with him. I didn't want to be a virgin anymore. I wanted to prove I'm a woman. I'm so sorry, mom. Forgive me, God forgive me."

"The devil is a liar, Sunday Summer. Don't you talk suicide again, do you hear me? Honey, one day you will meet the right guy and it will be glorious. I know because I waited on your dad to find me. I, too, was in love with a guy –named Dave Carter. He swept me off my feet at the age of fourteen. My mom kept a close watch on us. One day I saw him kissing a girl named Annie, and the next day he was kissing a girl named Carol. I cried a bucket of tears. I didn't have an interest in boys again until I met your dad – and now look at us. We have you and the boys. God has blessed us. You will get over it, Sunday, I promise you."

"Mom, thanks for that talk. I'm not going to commit suicide. I shouldn't have said that. What was I thinking? I don't want to go down as a statistic. I'm better than that and I'm stronger than some weak, crying, wimpy woman. Mom, I really appreciate all that you and dad teach me. Please don't tell either of my grandparents. I just want this to stay between us three."

"Between us three?" Clarice asks.

"Yes, mom. God, you and me."

Clarice laughs. "Sunday, you are so funny. Come give your mom a big hug. I love you, little girl. Do you know how much? I don't want to see you like this anymore. Let's go on a mother and daughter shopping spree. It will do you good."

"Mom, I have so much schoolwork. I will take you up on that shopping spree soon. I do need some new clothes. Thanks a lot mom. I love you, too."

"Okay Sunday, let me know when you're ready to go shopping. We'll go to New York City, where there are some nice different styles for you. Besides, I could use some new clothes myself."

Sunday hugs her mom. "Mom, I'm going to live for God and wait on my true love. I want him to be like my dad."

"Wait on God, Sunday. Wait on the Lord and be of good courage."

CHAPTER 5

Girl, You Better Watch Out

As Sunday celebrates her seventeenth birthday with her girlfriends, Avery walks up to her.

"Hi Sunday, I tried to call you to apologize, but you changed your number."

"Hi Avery, I thought you would be with your fiancé, Angie."

"Sunday, listen, Angie left me after you came over to the house that day. She said that I loved you more than her. And I do, Sunday."

"Avery, stop the lies that don't even sound right."

"Sunday, I'm not lying. She moved back to Texas with her parents. She left the college and said I was a two timer."

"Well, Avery, what else would someone call you?"

"Sunday, what do you want from me? Baby, I want another chance. Can we talk?"

"Avery, I'm here celebrating with my friends. This is not a good time. I'll call you tomorrow after my classes."

"Well, Sunday, can I get a kiss or a hug right here in front of your friends? I really miss you with your pretty smile and face."

"Stop it, Avery, I said I'll call you tomorrow. I have to go. My dad is picking me up in ten minutes." She bids her friends goodbye and walks away from the table.

"Sunday, please can we start over? I promise it'll be different this time."

"Avery, I am afraid to trust you again. You broke my heart. You will never ever get the chance to do it again. Now please leave before my dad shows up."

"Sunday, you know I would never disrespect you."

"Oh really? Listen, if you don't hear anything else I say, hear this. You will never get a chance to hurt me ever again. We can talk and be friends – that's all. Remember the morning I came over to your house?"

"Sunday, baby, of course I do."

"Well, I was going to give myself to you, but you had another woman living with you all the time."

42

"Angie and I were not living together. She told you that fiancé stuff to scare you off and you went for it."

"Man, what? I went for it. You didn't deny that she was your woman. Remember you said you were going to tell me, huh? You just stood there, looking surprised. Well, surprise, I ain't going to give myself to you or no other man. Do I make myself clear, Avery? I'm going to go to college, be a doctor and live a good life like my parents do."

"And I can give you that good life, Sunday. Please find it in your heart to forgive me, baby love."

"Don't start that again, Avery. Here comes my dad, I have to go. See you around sometime."

"Sunday don't let it end this way – please. I won't give up on you. I won't."

"Bye Avery."

"Hi dad," Sunday says. "I had a lot of fun on my birthday."

Clark interrupts. "Sunday, was that the Avery guy you used to see standing there?"

"Yes. But before you start, listen. He was not with me. He happened to show up at the restaurant because Helena told him about my birthday celebration. I told him I could not see him ever again. He was talking to me, that's all. It was nothing."

"Sunday, I trust you, baby girl. Just be careful about these guys…they say stuff to lure you into a trap. And then you can't break free."

"Dad, I really did like him, but he proved to be a liar and a cheat and I can't forgive that."

"Listen honey, you have to learn to forgive, because that's God's law for us. Just don't get caught up again. Okay?"

"Yes, dad."

"Sunday, before I forget, happy birthday! And this car you didn't notice I'm driving is your birthday surprise that mom and I got for you."

"Dad! You and mom said you had a surprise for me…and I thought it was a new puppy. But a car? Oh dad, thank you, thank you. God, thank you for my parents."

"Sunday, you are welcome, honey. Now listen, you must be careful. Drive to school and home for now – and then you can go other places. You have to be careful and obey all traffic laws."

"Okay dad, I will. I will. I'm so excited. Thank you, dad."

CHAPTER 6

Remember What You Promised

Six months later, Sunday is driving when she sees Avery standing at a bus stop. She stops and rolls down the window. "Hi Avery. Long time no see."

"Yeah, what happened, Sunday? Happy belated birthday. You are getting older, I see."

"Yes, I know I said I would call you, but I thought it would be best if I didn't."

"Sunday, can you give me a ride home? This bus is taking such a long time and I have to prepare for my test on

Wednesday. I left my car home this morning in a hurry. What do you say?"

"Okay, get in. My parents bought me this car for my seventeenth birthday."

"That is so cool of them."

"Yes, I was so surprised. A car for my birthday. Right now, they only want me to drive to school and back home, and I intend to obey them. I shouldn't be taking another route to take you home. But it is getting late."

"Thanks a lot. I really appreciate it. Listen, when can we talk about us again?"

"Avery, I told you I'm not dating right now. I have goals and plans in my life and you are not a part of them. I'm graduating in a few months; I'm excited and so are my parents. I've been accepted to

Harvard University. I'm not interested in being serious now."

"Really? You used to be when you talked about us getting married. Now you've changed your mind? You must be seeing someone else."

"No, I'm not. I'm single, but I'm careful. I'm glad I listened to my mom. She told me to wait to date and not to give myself to the first man I meet. She was right. I trusted you and you lied to me, Avery. I loved you so much, but you killed it, man."

"Listen, I will make it up to you, I promise. Angie is out of the picture."

"Avery, who mentioned her? Only you. See, you are so slick. I wanted you to meet my parents, but before I could plan that, you cheated on me. Tell me the truth. The two of you were seeing each other the whole time, right?"

"What? No! That's not right. Only when you turned me down...I just needed to be with someone. I've been going through some personal things from back home. My parents are talking divorce. It really hurt me and I just needed to hold someone that night. You weren't there. You showed up the next morning."

"I would have preferred to hold you, but you walked away from me. I'm so sorry about your parents. I'll pray for them, okay? My parents would break my heart, too, if they were going to divorce. Oh Avery, you must be heartbroken. Listen, I'll call you later after I finish my homework."

"I'm home. Well, why don't you come in and do your homework here. I can help you. No, I don't think so, you are playing on my emotions right now. Please just get out. You're home now. I have to be home at a certain time and I don't want to be disobedient to my parents."

"Sunday, I'm sorry. I didn't mean to touch your emotions like that. I just needed someone to talk to. Angie and I never had sex. She was just there for me to talk to. Stop the lies, Avery. She was in her nightgown and you were in the bathroom with a towel wrapped around you. Please, just get out. I have to go."

"It wasn't what you think. She wanted to and I said no because I love only you. She slept on the sofa. For real, Sunday. I only saw her in a nightgown when I woke up that morning."

"So, you're saying she put it on while you were asleep and you saw it later? Liar. Get out of my car."

"Sunday, believe me. I didn't even know she brought a nightgown with her when I asked her to come talk with me. I just needed her to talk to, not have sex with. Listen, I'm telling you the truth."

"Let me explain all that to you. You know you made love to her after telling me that you would wait until marriage. I told you I wanted to wait for marriage. Liar get out. I'm getting upset. Get out now."

Avery touches Sunday's hand. "I'm so sorry."

"Avery, get out. Now."

"Sunday, I'm sorry. Angie and I did have sex once that night because of my emotional state. Please call me so we can talk," he says, getting out of the car. "I miss you so much. Believe me, I do."

"I'll call you later after I finish my homework. Have a good evening."

Sunday walks into her house. "Hi everyone, I'm going to my room to get ready for dinner."

"Oh honey, I'm so glad you are home," Clarice says. "Dad and I were a little worried. You're usually home by now."

"I know. I dropped off a friend and we got to talking and the conversation got interesting. What's for dinner? I'm starved. Where are Clark and Calvin?"

"They went to karate practice with your dad, and they're going to stop for pizza. So, it's just you and I for dinner. Is that okay?"

"Yes, mom, that's fine."

"Sunday, you seem a little upset. Talk to me. Please honey, I don't want you to feel like you can't talk to me. I'm your mother. You saw Avery tonight, didn't you? Is he the friend you gave a ride to? Talk to me. I won't tell your dad, I promise. You look like you've been crying. Talk to me please."

"Yes, mom, it was Avery. He told me about his parents."

"What happened to them?"

"He said they are going through a divorce and he is really suffering from it. He said he had the other girl there for comfort."

"Sounds like a good excuse, Sunday, but don't you believe that lie. Men will say anything to get you feeling sorry for them and then the next thing you know, you will be comforting him in the bed."

"Mom, I'm not going to sleep with him or any other guy. I did love him, but my feelings toward him have changed. I can't stand for someone to just outright lie for no reason. He admitted that he slept with Angie and said it only happened once. I don't believe that. Mom, I saw a ring on her left hand, but I never questioned him. I believe they are engaged."

"Where is Angie now? Has she disappeared and gone South? That's another good lie men tell."

"He says she moved to Texas because of her finding out about me."

"The devil is a liar, Sunday. He is lying to you to get you in a compromising position. That girl is probably running from him…or she went home to have her baby."

"Oh! Mom, she wasn't pregnant. I saw her. I don't know why she left, but I do know he is a liar. Now I really won't call him tonight."

"He wants you to call him so he can play on your emotions more and more. When he gets you in a vulnerable place, he will convince you to sleep with him. Sunday, be careful for nothing."

"I didn't think about that. I'm supposed to call him after dinner. Should I or should I ignore him?"

"I can't stop you from being his friend, but I will tell you again to be careful for nothing. Don't keep giving him rides home; he will use that as much as he can. Tell him that you can't. As sure as I'm your mom, he will try to lure you into his apartment. Next, he'll break down and cry to play on your emotions. Girl, don't you get caught up after you've been warned. Avery is playing the 'I need you as my friend' game with you.

Listen, baby, don't put him to the test. You may not be strong enough to push him away once he gets you in his apartment. Stay from there, do you hear? I'm talking from experience, not from what I read in a book or what someone told me. My mom warned me and I learned to listen and take heed – and that's why I have a life with your dad today."

"Mom, you're scaring me. Yes, I hear you loud and clear."

Clark walks in. "What do you hear loud and clear, Sunday? You two okay?" He kisses Clarice on the lips lightly, then kisses Sunday on the forehead.

"Yes, honey, we were talking about an issue on one of Sunday's topics about marriage and relationships. How was your pizza party with the boys?"

"Just great, honey," Clark says. "Those guys can eat. We ordered three pizzas and they ate most of it. I just had two slices. I want some of what you cooked…oh, my favorite! Meatloaf, mashed potatoes, string beans, gravy. Where are the hot biscuits, Clarice?"

Clarice shakes her head, smiling. "They are in the oven cooking. I'll get you a plate, honey."

"I'm starving for your home cooking. Sunday, how was your day, honey? How are you enjoying your car? Is it running okay?"

"It's brand new, dad. It's running fine. And my day was interesting, I must say, but better since I spoke with mom. I heard you talk about all that pizza...my brothers must be stuffed. Where are they?"

"Baby girl, they went to their room to do homework. I sure hope they don't fall asleep after all that pizza and soda. I let them enjoy themselves. They had very good grades this term."

59

"Dad, you're the greatest dad ever. Listen, maybe you and I can have pizza one day. I only want two slices though. After two slices, I'm full to the brim."

"Excuse me, Sunday," Clark interrupts, turning to Clarice. "Honey, did you see the bag I left on the table in the living room?"

"No, I didn't see a bag. I'll go look, just hold tight."

"No honey, you sit. I'll go get it," Clark says, getting up from the table. He comes back and hands Clarice the bag. "Here you are. Open it, baby."

"Oh Clark, it is so beautiful! A diamond necklace and earrings?"

"Yes honey, anything for my darling wife. I love you, Clarice. I'm glad you're my wife and friend," he says, kissing her.

"Dad, they are so beautiful," Sunday says. "You are the best of the best dads and the greatest. Oh dad, you really love mom…and that makes me want to wait on a man like you."

"You better. Listen Sunday, when a man loves a woman, he doesn't wait for a birthday, Valentine's Day, or some other holiday to bless and appreciate her. I love your mom and when I see something I want to give her, I buy it in the spirit of the moment. Love is showed in deeds – remember that. A real man wants nothing but the best for his lady love. Keep that in mind when you meet the man of your dreams. He will find you and you both will know it's God's doing."

Clarice kisses Clark on the lips softly. "I love you, Clark Summer."

"Okay you two, you are getting too mushy," Sunday says. "Let us pray over this food before dinner is canceled. Mom, dad, you're the best. I love you both."

Sunday Summer
Someone to Love Me...

PART TWO

INTRODUCTION

Part Two

Many are waiting on or looking for love. Often, we get anxious, we can't wait on God, and we miss the red flags. We become infatuated by that handsome face, that deep voice, that swag walk he has, and his fine suits and ties...looking like he belongs in *GQ Magazine*. Don't let the outer appearance fool you, girls. Check out his personality and attitude. Check out his work history. Does Mr. Good Looking have a steady job? Can he support a family, or does he spend all his money on himself as he tries to dress to impress? Does he anger quickly?

How is his temper when you show up late for that dinner date because you had to find a babysitter or work an hour late? If he does anger quickly, is he a striker or an abuser? All these things need to be considered. Some women have children and need to make sure they are secure before they leave them, but good guys don't mind. A good guy is patient, kind and understanding to his woman. He'll love you and your child.

Read your Bibles and don't ever forget what the Word of God says: *"Whoso findeth a wife findeth a good thing, and obtaineth favor of the LORD."* Does he know about your belief in God, or is he an atheist? You've got to find these things out, ladies. You don't want to fall into a trap that you can't easily get out of. Is he willing to attend church with you or take you to his church? When my daughter Linda was dating a guy, she immediately took him to church with her to meet her pastor. Pastors have discernment and can help you know if this guy is a loser or a winner. You don't want a loser, because he will use you for all that he can get. Does he make sexual remarks to you? Does he pay for the meal or ask you to pay because his payday is next week? And don't accept the sad story: "I've got to find a place to move into...my landlord wants the apartment." That's shacking up. Don't do it. Don't put yourself out there like that, girl. Watch the red flags, ladies.

The Scriptures let us know that we are a blessing to the man that findeth us and he will receive God's favor. It sounds like God knows what's best for us women. If we go out on our own, forcing marriage or initiating it ourselves, we are taking a chance on heartbreak and depression. So, I would like to say this to you: wait on God. Pray, read your Bible, and be anxious for nothing. He will strengthen you to be able to wait and prepare yourself for your man. Remember that Queen Esther had to go through a year of preparation in order to have one night with the King. So, when you meet your king, baby girl, you are going to be wonderfully blessed.

Love, *Evangelist Anne*

CHAPTER 7

Someone to Love Me

Sunday seems happy enough. She has a new car and will attend college in the fall. Her parents are excited for her, but her brothers are going to miss her reading to them and helping them with their schoolwork. Sunday has her life all planned out. She has been accepted to Harvard University, her dream school, she is planning to become a pediatrician, and she has a long road ahead of her.

She is praying about Avery because he won't stop messaging her; she is troubled, but afraid to tell her dad. She says she doesn't want any trouble, so she ignores Avery's advances and avoids driving by his bus stop, but she still cares a lot for him.

I would generally say this is a good way to get rid of a guy you want to avoid; but what happens when he won't give up the game? You have to get away quickly before you forget about the heartthrobs and cunning words that lured you in the first time. The game is still the same – and while sometimes there are different players, many times they're the same. Girls, watch out, because your future is at stake. Oh, I would have loved to warn Sunday.

While Sunday is in the library studying, Avery approaches her. "Hi Sunday, my one and only love, how are you today?"

"Sheesh, we're in the library, Avery. What is it?"

Avery stares at Sunday. "I just can't believe how beautiful you are. You really touch my heart with your sexy style."

"Avery, please don't do that. I told you we can't be together anymore. Now please be quiet, I'm trying to study."

"Please come outside, I need to speak with you. It's important."

Sunday thinks for a moment and sighs. "Give me a minute to put my books away." She feels a bit out of sorts but wants to hear what Avery has to say and goes outside. "Avery, what is it? I need to go home so I can study. What is so urgent? I don't have long to talk because I have finals all this week."

"Sunday, I heard from your girlfriend Elisah that you were accepted into Harvard. Congratulations."

"Thanks, Avery, I am truly excited about going. You'll be graduating from college and I'll be in my first year of my new life as a college student."

"I'm going to miss you, girl, but we'll stay in contact somehow."

"Maybe God will bring us back together again after we reach our life goals."

"Yes, Sunday, that is true. How time flies and then we are apart for how long? Listen, want to stop off and have a chocolate milkshake, Sunday? I know that's your favorite. It's my treat. What do you say?"

"Okay," Sunday says, caught up in the moment. How her heart beats fast when he is around. "I have about an hour to kill before I'm due home. You are driving now, I see. Do I leave my car here or follow you?"

"Follow me since you have to get home early. I don't want you to be late getting home. We're going over to the Webb Shack. Okay?"

"Okay, Avery. I'm following you."

Avery leads the way and Sunday follows. After they arrive at the restaurant, they walk inside hand in hand. Sunday has forgotten to be careful.

"Good evening, sir, you have a table for two," the waiter says.

"We prefer a booth," says Avery.

"Sure, follow me," the waiter says. "You and the young lady can sit here. She is a pretty girl, man."

"Yes, she is, thank you. I think so too."

"Avery, something is troubling you," Sunday says. "I pray all is okay with your mom and dad."

"My mom is fine. She hopes dad will come back home after he finishes spreading his wild oats at fifty-nine years old. My dad filed for divorce and that's breaking my mom's heart, but she is holding on to faith. I went to visit her the week before last. She cried on my shoulder, but then she smiled and said, 'God will have His way in this.' She has accepted the fact that they may never rekindle their relationship. Baby, I don't want that to happen to us. I would be crushed."

"Oh Avery, how devastating for your mother. We will continue praying for her. Is there anyone there to check on her?"

"My sister is there with her and that's a blessing. I really thank God for her staying with mom at a time like this."

"Did you see your dad at all while you were home?"

"Yes, I spoke to dad. He said that he still loves mom, but that he fell in love with someone else. He said he feels bad about hurting mom, but he has to go with his heart."

"Oh wow, man, what a bad feeling I just got."

"Sunday, what happened? You looked so sad for a moment. And you are tearing up."

"I thought about how you and I loved each other and then that other woman opened your door, saying she was your fiancé. Men change their minds in an instant. I can't do this, Avery," Sunday says, getting up to leave.

"Wait, please," Avery says, touching her hand. She sits back down. "Sunday, it is you who I love, not anyone else. Don't compare what we can have with my parents...please don't. I will always love you. I have from the beginning."

"You say that now, but think about what happened in just that moment because I refused to give myself to you?"

75

"You said you came over that day to give yourself to me, did you?"

"I did. I was angry with my mom for slapping me so hard because I spoke up to her, but I'm glad I discovered the situation. You hurt me so bad, Avery, and I'm afraid to trust you now. I'm just not ready to be heartbroken again. I know we all need someone to love us. But I want a sincere, loyal, and truthful man who can love me like my dad loves my mother. Someone to love me is important."

"Don't let that one mistake keep us apart. I really need you by my side. I want us to get married someday and have our own family."

"Do you really mean that? Because I've never stopped loving you," Sunday says, crying.

"Come here, Sunday. Just hold me close to you," Avery says, crying and wiping his eyes. "I need you. Please give us another chance."

"Avery, you're crying," Sunday says. She wipes his eyes with her hand and holds him. One thing turns into another. "Avery, let's go to your place so we can be alone. I can't stand to see you so sad."

Perhaps Avery is really feeling sad - or maybe Sunday is playing into the hands of a liar. When they reach Avery's apartment, he says, "Come on in. Would you like a glass of soda or water?"

"No, I just want to talk to you, encourage you to be strong, and pray for your parents. I really have to leave in about thirty minutes or so. My mom and dad need me to watch my brothers because they have tickets to a Broadway play."

"Aren't Clark and Calvin older now? Do they need a babysitter?"

"Well, not really, but I want to be there with them so mom and dad don't have to worry and can enjoy themselves. Children can get into a lot when left alone."

"Yeah, I guess you are right. Well, I better make good use of these thirty minutes. Take a look around. I'm not such a bad housekeeper, am I? I decorated myself and picked out all the colors. I would have loved if you'd done the coloring for me, but I did what needed to be done to make it home."

Sunday picks up a framed picture. "Avery, who is this? She is so beautiful. What's her name?"

"Oh, that's my baby sister. She's the one staying with my mom. She is beautiful like you, Sunday."

"I would love to meet her someday."

"You will. I was thinking about inviting you to meet my family this year at our family reunion."

"Really? I would love to meet your family, especially your mom. Let me know so I can make plans."

Time flies.

"Avery, it's time for me to leave. I love you. Always remember that and don't be sad. But I really have to go home now."

"I'll call you later after your parents go out," Avery says, kissing her tenderly.

"Good night, Avery," Sunday says as she gets into her car. "Oh my, I have fifteen minutes to get home." *I wish I could stay with Avery to comfort his pain,* she thinks to herself. *Oh, I hate to have left him alone like that. He needs me and I can't be there for him like before. But I must be careful.*

When Sunday reaches home, Clarice calls out to her. "So glad you are home, honey. Hey, you okay? You look a little sad."

"No, I'm fine, I'm just thinking about something I have to do for class. Hey, you two have a good time. The boys will be fine. Don't worry."

"Honey, we'll see you when the show is over."

"Okay, enjoy your Broadway show."

As her parents leave, the phone rings. "Hi Avery, how are you? I have to get my brothers tucked in and I'll call you back. Give me about twenty minutes. Okay?"

She calls up to her brothers. "Hey you guys, it's almost time for your homework, so get busy. I'll be up there in about thirty minutes to check on you."

"Okay Sunday," Clark Jr. calls from upstairs.

Sunday has a flashback. *I'm not calling Avery,* she thinks. *I need to watch myself and remember how he hurt me before. I'm afraid of falling into that web again.*

"I'm coming up, guys," she calls to her brothers.

CHAPTER 8

Why Did I Come This Way?

Sunday has been receiving more texts from Avery lately than usual. He seems to be going through emotional distress now that his parents have finally divorced. He has been pressuring Sunday to talk with him because, as he says, she is the only one who can soothe his heart.

Sunday's phone rings. It's Avery. "Hello. Oh, it's you. I've been praying for you a lot, you know. I really feel terrible about your parents. Like I told you before, I would go to pieces if my parents divorced. Anyway, how are you coming along?"

"Oh Sunday, it hurts to the core of my being – and sometimes, I just feel like running so far away that no one can ever find me again," Avery says.

"Don't talk like that. Truly, God is able to deliver you from this hurt you're feeling. You have to accept it and go on with your life."

"If I had you to just hug me, I would feel better. I need you to be here with me right now."

"Avery, you know I can't do that. It's been forbidden by my parents. I have to be obedient to them…and more so to God. I told you a long time ago that I want to wait until marriage before I give myself to a man. But you seem to think that sex is the answer to every distress. It may make you feel good

84

for a moment, but what happens when it's over and the problem is still there? If sex was the answer to all of our issues, there would be a lot of healing in marriages and relationships. I disagree with you – me holding you won't make it better. Please stop saying that to try to entice me to sleep with you…because I won't."

"Listen, I didn't say that sex solves all problems and I'm not asking you to break your promise to God or your parents. I just want to hold you. I never told you to have sex with me."

"But all that hugging will lead to other things and you know it. Don't try to make me feel guilty because I have morals I intend to follow."

"I apologize. I should have said that if I could just see you, I would feel better. I would. I won't lie to you. I love you, Sunday. Whether you want to believe it or not, you are my soul mate. And I'm willing to wait."

"You mean you're willing to wait until I finish college and start my career? I don't believe that for one minute, man. You are used to having sex…and you pretend to be innocent, but I know different. Are you willing to wait on me? I know you're not, so stop it. In the waiting, you'll cheat on me with other women, and I can't do that to you or myself. I don't think that we should enter into another relationship. Why don't we just play it by ear, wait, and see what God does in our lives? We can still be friends."

"Listen, I have to go. It's time for me to go to work – and I have a late class this evening. We'll talk soon, okay? Thanks for the conversation."

"Okay, I'll talk to you later."

CHAPTER 9

How Do I Handle This?

Sunday walks into her kitchen. "Mom, I need to speak to you. Where are you?"

"Hi honey! I'm here. I was in the laundry room. Is everything okay?"

"Mom, I don't want you to get upset and tell dad."

"Sunday, what is wrong? Are you okay, honey?"

"Yeah, I just need to speak with you about something I'm experiencing."

"Okay, let's sit down. Now tell me what's wrong."

"It's not that something is wrong. I just have an issue that is troubling me...concerning Avery."

"Okay, that's enough. You aren't seeing him again, are you? We forbid you from seeing that young man. You said that you caught him with another woman! Don't put yourself through unnecessary heartache, baby."

"Mom, listen. He called me today. He is going through some stress because his parents have divorced. The issue is...he says that seeing me will make him better. But I don't want to get caught up in a moment with him."

"Then don't. Avery is playing on your emotions – and you have a future that you are working towards. Don't get involved with him, baby. Please don't. You'll be sorry if you do."

"Mom, that's why I'm talking to you and not to dad. I just wanted to know if, well…did you ever experience this with a boy when you were my age?"

"I had my heart broken by a boy at a young age when I didn't know anything about love. He tried to control my feelings, but I did just what you are doing. I spoke to my mom and she advised me to stay clear of him. So that's my same advice to you. Block him off your phone. Concentrate on the Lord, baby girl. Love will come and it will be sweet and sincere and worth the wait. I promise you. Look at your dad and me! Stop looking for someone to love you. Love finds its own way."

"Mom, I do love him, but I'm not ready to be in a sexual relationship with him. I told him that, but I know he really don't hear me. What should I do? How can I still be his friend?"

"Befriend him at a distance. Okay?"

"Mom don't worry. I'll take your advice. But can this stay just between us?"

"Okay, as long as you promise me that you will be careful."

"I promise, mom," Sunday says, hugging her. "Thanks."

Though Sunday intends to keep her promise, her heart seems to keep getting in the way. Knowing her mixed feelings about him, Avery continues to push Sunday – he knows where her weak spots are and he seeks to use them to his advantage.

The phone rings. *Oh, Avery's calling again*, Sunday thinks to herself. *Lord, how do I handle this? My heart is going so fast, and it scares me. I feel so much love for Avery and it's wrecking my mind. I have to concentrate on my finals…I'm graduating this year. Lord, help me.*

"Hello Avery!"

"Hi, my love. How are you feeling today? I miss you so much."

"I'm on my way out to run some errands. I have to find a luggage set so I can start packing some things for college, and then I have to meet my mom later. We're going shopping for some new clothes for me. Avery, I'm so excited about going away to college."

"Yeah, I'm going to miss you baby. Can I see you today? Can you fit me into your schedule? It sounds like you have a busy itinerary today."

"Yes, Avery, it is busy for me."

"Wow Sunday, can a guy see his main girl for a minute?"

"I want to see you, but I'm busy."

Avery changes the subject. "Sunday, how is your mom doing? Ask her to pray for me please. And please pray for my mom. She's so distraught. The divorce is final and my dad told her he's marrying his newfound love. Mom just sulks all the time."

"Oh, Avery. I pray she bounces back soon. How could he hurt her like that? Men always pretend like they love you, and then when a new face comes along, there they go…gone with her and leaving her hurt. I will keep her in prayer."

"Thanks baby. Hey, want to grab a burger and milkshake for a minute? That is, if you are coming out this way to shop. I sure could use the support after speaking with my mom."

"Okay, I'm on my way that way. Meet me at Salson Café so we can talk a little more. I can't see you for long because I have to meet my mom at 2pm."

" I appreciate any time you give me, Sunday."

"See you soon," Sunday says, hanging up. The phone rings again. "Hi mom. No, I didn't forget I have to meet you at 2 o'clock. I'll see you then."

Sunday walks into the café. Avery stands up to greet her. "Hey Sunday, over here! Girl, you sure look beautiful. I really love you. Let's get married today…elope."

"Avery, stop it. You know we can't do that."

"Yeah, but I would if you just say so. How you doing, beautiful woman of mine?"

"Stop it. We are just friends, remember?"

"I know, but I am claiming you for mine…I love you, Sunday.

"I'm off to college in a few months. I told you we have to wait and see how things go."

"Okay, don't get upset with me. I don't want you to walk away."

"I only have 30 minutes. It's 1:30 and I promised mom I would meet her at 2pm. Maybe we can meet later. I have some time tonight. My brothers have karate class, so I don't have to help with homework."

"Okay, call me when you want to meet up. "

"I was thinking maybe we could have a movie night at your house so we can talk some more about our future. You've been sounding so serious lately. Are you really, Avery?"

"Of course I am, girl. I just want us to be together one day. Forever. Without anyone coming between us. But Sunday… you have some pretty strict stuff you are governed by."

"Wait a minute now, I'm not governed by stuff. Yes, I help my brothers out. I love them. I've always helped them with homework and I like to hang out with them sometimes. They're my brothers. They're all I have. That shouldn't take away from my relationship with you. Or does it?"

"Well no, it's just that you are so dedicated to them. I just want some quality time with you too."

"That's not so easy right now...I'm also studying a lot. That's why I'm not sure if this relationship with us will work. I want to pass my classes with straight A's and be part of honor society. It's always been that way. I'm not sacrificing my study time for anyone except the Lord. And that means making time for church, bible study and

97

prayer. That is essential for me to have a close relationship with God. That's something else we need to talk about. Are you praying like you should and reading your Bible as you ought to?"

"Yes, yes, I am. Just not as much as you. But I talk to God all the time about you and me."

"We all have to give Him quality time and be unwavering. Anyway, what time do you want me to come to your place? I can't let my parents know. They aren't too keen on me seeing you because of what happened the last time. But I know you've changed. I guess what's happening with your mom has made you a more dedicated man. At least I feel that way. Don't let me be wrong, Avery. I have to tell them if we are dating again, okay? I like to be honest with my parents, especially my mom."

"Sunday girl, I'm not asking you to lie. When can I meet your parents so they will know that I'm serious about you and willing to wait until you get your education?"

"I don't know. They're a little skeptical about me dating you. So, I would rather they meet you as my friend and we can just keep our dating between us. Okay?"

"Whatever you want, Sunday. Whatever you say, I'll do. I just want to keep you as my one and only love forever."

"Don't make me blush, Avery. You sure have a way with words. What do you want to talk about?"

"Well, I'd prefer to just sit and look at your pretty face for thirty minutes. That'll be all right with me."

Sunday hits him playfully. "Okay then, you just sit and look at me," she says, laughing.

"Now you are making me blush, Sunday. Hey, do you want me to cook you something good to eat? I can cook, you know."

"Well what is your favorite dish to prepare? And it better not be a TV dinner."

Avery laughs. "Baked chicken a la Avery with asparagus tips, carrots, and baked potato with sour cream – oh, and ice cream."

"Okay, I like that. Are you going to have time to do all that cooking? It seems like a task to me."

"I'll stop by the supermarket and get what I need and when you show up, it'll be done. Watch. Okay, see you around 7:30."

" Listen, I've got to be going, mom is waiting. Love you, Avery."

"Love you back, Sunday."

CHAPTER 10

Play with Fire and You'll Get Burned

Sunday walks up to Clarice. "Hey mom! You ready to run up dad's credit cards girl shopping?"

"Sure am! How about you?" Clarice says, kissing Sunday on the cheek. "Hey Sunday, I like that glow on your face. You are so radiant, honey. Did you run into an angel that told you how beautiful you are?"

"No mom, I'm always radiant. You are such a great mom and I love being with you. When I go off to college, I'm going to miss you and all of our girls shopping days and movie times. I love you so much, mom."

"And I love you, Sunday. Hey, I saw this store that has some great jeans and shirts right over there."

"Let the spending begin."

Sunday and Clarice shop for hours. When it begins to get dark, Clarice says, "Are you hungry, Sunday?"

" No, not now. I'm going out to study later and I'll have something then. Oh, it's 6 o'clock! We better be heading home before dad sends out the troops for us."

When they reach home, Clark greets them. "How was shopping for my two favorite girls? I know my credit card is maxed out!"

"No, Sunday was very careful not to do that. And I was too," says Clarice. "Hey, how about we have a night for just husband and wife? The boys are with grandma and grandpa and Sunday is going out to study."

"Sounds good to me. I can order some pizza. Or do you want something else?"

"Pizza sounds like fun."

"Okay, I'll order it now."

As Clarice joins Sunday in the kitchen, Sunday says, "Mom, I really love the relationship you and dad have. I pray that I can have that for myself someday."

"Sunday, it will happen. Trust God, baby, and it will happen – and it will be sweet and anointed. Let God ordain who your mate is and it will be everlasting. You will have ups and downs, but that's part of being happily married to the one true love of your life."

"I can't wait," Sunday says, hugging her. "Thanks mom. I'm leaving for study time. Enjoy your night with dad."

Sunday calls Avery and says, "Hi, I'm getting ready. How is dinner coming along? I'll see you in a few."

After Sunday arrives at Avery's house, she rings the doorbell. Avery opens the door and greets her. "Hi baby girl, come on in. Dinner is almost ready for the lady love of my life. Here, come sit here at the table. Your appetizer is ready."

"Avery, this table setting is beautiful. Did you do this just for me?"

"Yes, my love, only for you. I made miniature crab cakes, lobster tails and oysters for our appetizer – and afterward we can have a salad. For dinner, I made chicken a la Avery with garlic asparagus and baked potatoes with sour cream and cheese. For dessert, we'll have my favorite strawberry cheesecake topped with whipped cream. I couldn't find my favorite ice cream. We also have homemade lemonade to drink. And after dinner, we can have some wine. How does that sound, love?"

"Sounds like I'm hungry! But Avery, I don't drink wine. Does it have alcohol in it?"

Avery looks surprised. "Girl, the Bible says a little wine is good for the stomach. It only has 13 percent alcohol in it. It won't make you feel woozy, I promise. Trust me, Sunday, I will never do anything to damage our relationship. I love you." Avery kisses her gently and carefully.

"Okay, I trust you. Well, let's eat and enjoy this dinner. I could get used to this, man. Avery, please the blessing."

"Father, we thank you for this meal from your bountiful harvest. Let it give nourishment to our bodies – in Jesus name."

"You pray like my dad does. Thank you. Enjoy your meal."

"Well, I intend to be a good husband and a great dad to our children."

"Avery, that's the future, not now. You're acting like a man with a child already."

"What does that mean? Why can't I trust in God for our future life together?"

" I don't want to argue with you, Avery. I just made a statement. I know you will make a great dad to our children someday. I trust that you remember what I said and that you won't force me to do anything against what I believe. I know some girls are anxious to lay with the guys they are supposedly in love with, but I want to wait. I'm a virgin and I want to stay that way until we hear 'you may kiss the bride.' Okay?"

"I hear you loud and clear. I hear you and I respect that. What time do you have to be home? I don't want to let anything stop me from seeing you again."

"I can stay out until twelve."

"Okay, it's 8 o'clock, so I'll have you for at least three and a half hours. Wow! I'm a blessed man."

After they finish dinner, they retire to living room. "Sunday, what would you like to do? Maybe watch TV or listen to some music? It's your choice."

"I would prefer some nice soft music."

"Come Sunday, dance with me," Avery says, putting on the song "Always and Forever" like the experienced man he is. "We never danced to a love song before. At least let me hold you in my arms."

"This is one of my favorite songs. I want this song sung at our wedding. It has so much love in the words," Sunday says, looking up at Avery. "I really love you, Avery, I do. I love you so much."

Avery holds her close. "I love you too, Sunday. Come, let's sit and drink a little dinner wine. I have something that I want to say to you."

"What's wrong? Is your mom okay?"

"Yes, she's okay. It's about us. I have to go to Texas for a couple of weeks during winter break, and I want us to spend a weekend together before I go."

"Avery, I can't do that," Sunday says. "My parents will be furious."

"Tell them that you are going on a senior trip. They don't check behind you. I want to take you to a couple's retreat. You're eighteen now, Sunday. You should not have to ask permission from them about

110

everything. Why can't you go with me? It'll be a good experience for us as a couple."

"First of all, you just told me to lie to them. I'm not doing that. I will think and pray about the trip, how's that?"

"Well, it's just that it's next week."

"What? Next week! Oh, I really have to think about that, honey."

Avery goes over to his desk and pulls out some brochures. "Read these. They offer horseback riding, workshops for engaged couples, and building relationships seminars. They have great speakers. Say you'll go with me. I'm sorry I told you to lie to your parents...forgive me."

"I forgive you, sweetie. Yes, I'll go. I'll tell them that I'm taking a trip for winter break. They won't question me. Listen, it's getting late and I have to go home. Would you get my jacket, please?"

Avery gets her jacket for her and says, "Okay, let me walk you to your car. Be safe and call me when you get in the house."

"Okay, I will, " Sunday says, kissing Avery goodnight.

Sunday happily drives home, singing. She can't wait to spend a weekend with her one true love. He seems trustworthy – and she's pleased that he told her she can trust him. But trust is only to be put in God. Sunday is taking Avery at his word, but she doesn't realize that Avery has a different agenda for their weekend getaway. Young ladies always tell your parents or someone else where you are going, with whom you are going, and where you're going – even if

112

it is with your boyfriend. The devil has many plots, tricks and plans set up for you. Let's see what happens with Sunday and Avery. Oh, what a wicked web we weave – and whoever gets caught in it is the victim.

CHAPTER 11

A Surprise Phone Call

In the morning, Sunday is happy. She kisses her mom on the cheek. "Good morning, mother. Where are dad and the boys?"

"They went to karate class. The boys have a tournament and they wanted dad to go with them to see their moves. You know how men are unpredictable. The boys told me to tell you that they are giving you a break from taking them."

"So, what are we going to do today?"

"Unfortunately, I have a meeting at church with the communion committee. It will be about two hours long because I'm training the new servers. What are you going to do, Sunday?"

"I'll just go do some online shopping. Actually, I know! I'll go to the mall. I saw something there I want to get for school."

"Okay, enjoy yourself I'll see you later," Clarice says, walking out the door. The phone rings. "Summer's residence, may I help you?"

A familiar voice says, "Hi, may I speak to Miss Sunday Summer?"

"Yes, this is she. Who am I speaking with?"

"Hi Sunday, this is Denzel Thomason. We met at the college fair last year in Massachusetts. We dated for a while. Do you remember me?" Denzel asks, laughing.

"Oh, yes! How are you doing, Denzel? It's been a long time since I've spoken to you. I thought you lost my number. After you went off to college, we lost contact. Did I do something wrong? Or what happened?"

"No, you didn't. I wanted to talk with you about our relationship, but things got a bit of out of sorts after I moved to Massachusetts – where I reside now. How could I ever forget a young woman as lovely as you? I was thinking about the beautiful dinner we had at the Oasis Restaurant before I left for college. I really wanted to come visit you and spend time with you, but I lost your number. Anyway, I'm teaching at Harvard this year and I was hoping you chose it to be your college."

"Yes, I'm attending this August. I didn't know you were teaching there! I thought you were an undergrad student."

"I was hired this year and I saw your acceptance letter. I thought to myself that I had to give you a call. I didn't know if you decided to go somewhere else. Sometimes we change our mind and go other places. By the way, are you involved with someone special? I don't want to overstep my bounds. I know we never really were steady since your parents didn't want you dating so early. But after I told you I'm waiting on you; I lost my phone with your number."

"To answer your question, yes and no. I am dating someone named Avery but, God willing, I'll be at Harvard in July to sign papers and get my housing together. Avery and I have to wait until I finish college to have a more serious relationship, so I don't know how it's going to work out when I come there."

"Okay, well I'll see you when you come in July then. Keep my number so we can stay in touch."

"I will. Thanks for calling me. Bye Denzel."

Oh wow, he remembered me, Sunday thinks to herself. *And now he is a teacher! Oh yeah, he is 23 years old, so I guess he graduated last year. I'm excited to have a friend there.* Sunday then goes off to the mall to shop.

When Sunday returns home, she walks in and asks, "What's for dinner? I'm

118

starving. Oh mom! You made my favorite – baked lasagna and salad."

"How was your shopping today? Did you buy anything?" Clarice asks.

Clark interrupts. "Can you two do the girl talk after dinner? I want to give a praise report. The boys came in first place and won a trophy in karate black belt! I'm so proud of them. The boys wanted McDonalds on the way home, so that's why they aren't at the dinner table. They were both tired and they're now sound asleep! Let's eat." After Clark prays, he says, "Okay, pass the lasagna dish. I'm starving too! Sunday, I was thinking about you, baby. Soon you will be headed off to Harvard! I pray that you will meet the man of your dreams there and that Avery stays far away from there."

119

"Clark, stop it honey," Clarice says. "Avery is finishing undergrad school here and then going back to Texas. Right, Sunday?"

"I don't know his future plans, but whatever he decides he is still my friend," Sunday says. "Dad, why are you so hard on Avery? He is a nice person and I am very fond of him."

"Sunday, he's not the one for you," Clark says. "He is a liar and he plays tricks with women. I know how he hurt you, baby girl. Your dad is only concerned about you, baby."

"Daddy, I appreciate it, but lighten up, okay? Anyway, I'm going away next weekend. I'm leaving Friday afternoon and I'll be back Sunday. I'm taking a vacation before college. I'll call you when I get there."

"Just be careful and watchful, okay honey?"

"I will, dad."

"Well, ladies, I'm retiring to the TV to watch SWAT. You girls clean up the dishes," Clark says as he leaves the room.

"Okay dad, we got it."

"Sunday, you know how your dad is about Avery," Clarice says. "So, don't take it personally. You have to understand that he is a man who believes in family values."

"I know mom, I know. Well, since we're all finished, I'm going to retire to my room. Goodnight."

"Goodnight Sunday. Sleep well."

As Sunday heads to her room, Clarice remembers that she wants to ask Sunday who is she going on vacation with and where she will be going. She decides to ask her in the morning.

CHAPTER 12

A Weekend to Forget

Sunday's secret weekend with Avery has finally arrived. Outside Avery's house, Sunday dials his number on her phone. "Hi Avery, I'm outside your door. Do you want to drive my car or yours? I have to park it in a garage otherwise."

"We can drive your car. I already parked mine in the garage for the weekend."

"Would you bring me an extra blanket in case they don't have enough?"

"Don't worry about being cold, Sunday, I'll keep you warm," Avery says, smiling.

Sunday blushes.

Avery gets into the car and kisses Sunday. "Sunday, I thought you were driving."

"No, you are. Don't you see I'm on the passenger side? Anyway, I brought us a couple sandwiches from the deli and some iced tea and potato chips. Will they be serving food this weekend or do we have to go out and fend for ourselves?"

"They'll have three meals a day and two snacks. And the first seminar starts at 8pm – so we have plenty of time, my darling."

"Okay. What is the topic for tonight?"

"It's called 'Building on what we have.' "

"Sounds good; that's what we're doing," Sunday says, touching his face. "I'm kind of excited about our getaway weekend. No one questioned me after I said that I was going on a weekend retreat. Mom probably figured it was about college. You know, I don't feel like I have to tell them everything. I'm 18 and can make sound decisions."

"You're right. And you are with a mature, 21-year-old man. I love you, Sunday girl."

"Avery, I didn't tell my parents that I was with you...I didn't think they would understand."

"Baby, you are in good hands – just like the Allstate insurance that covers this car. Relax! And stop worrying so much.

Also, I brought some wine and figured we can enjoy that with a nice movie tonight."

"Avery, can I ask you a question?"

"Sure, ask away."

"Who is my roommate for this retreat? I take for granted that the men and women who are single are living in different quarters."

"Why do you worry so much? I'm sick of you and your virginity issues. I got us a cabin together. But I will sleep on the sofa, okay? You are safe."

"Why are you talking to me in that manner?" Sunday asks, sounding worried.

"Because you are always bugging me out with, 'I want to wait until marriage.' "

"Well that's what I believe – and you can't change that. If we're not going to a resort, let me know and you can take me back home."

"Home?" Avery yells, upset. "We are 50 miles out of Poughkeepsie…and you are talking about going home? We only have about 10 more miles to go. If you had been reading the signs instead of worrying about your vagina issues, you would have known we're almost there."

"I'm sorry, Avery, but I don't have vagina issues – but it's mine and no one is going to take what I don't give freely. I'm not one of those free, loose women you screw around with. Listen, we are off to have a fun weekend. Let's not argue, it just makes me nervous. I see the Love Nest Retreat. Is that where we are going?"

"Yes."

"Okay, we're here. I'm sorry. I didn't mean to make you angry."

"I'm not angry. Let's just forget it and have the fun we came to have, okay?"

"Okay."

"You sit here and I'll go check us in. We are in cabin number 11. I'll go get the key."

"Okay, I'll wait here."

Lord, please keep me alert in every situation and help me not to drink too much wine if any at all, Sunday thinks to herself. *Lord, I see something in Avery that I've never seen before. And I'm feeling afraid. I should text mom and let her know where I am. No, how silly of me to think that. Avery wouldn't hurt me. Or would he? He did get really upset. Well, I'm glad this is my car. I will leave and return home if I need to. If dad finds out I'm here I'll be scolded and he will take my car back. Oh God, please forgive me...I should have told mom I was going here with Avery. I'll see how this works out tonight.*

"Hey Sunday, drive around the back to our cabin. I'm going to get our food vouchers."

Once at the cabin, Avery and Sunday unload their luggage. "This is so romantic," Sunday says as she looks around. "Look! We have a fireplace. This place is beautiful. Mom and dad would love this for their church function for married couples."

"Listen Sunday, we are registered as Mr. & Mrs. Avery and Sunday Thomas.

Don't answer any questions that noisy people ask."

"I won't, Avery. But I'm hungry. Let's go to the cafeteria." Looking around at all the food there, Sunday says, "I'm going to get stuffed. Avery was this expensive?"

"Not really. And you are worth it. It costs $500 per couple for two nights – and it's my treat."

After dinner, they attend the workshop and then return to their cabin.

"Sunday, you can take your shower first. I'll get us a little wine for the stomach's sake. Then we can sit by the fireplace and watch TV."

Nervous, Sunday goes to take her shower. To her surprise, Avery doesn't bother her. After she finishes, she walks back out to an empty room. "Avery, where are you?"

Avery opens the door. "I went out to get some ice from the machine. I'm going to take my shower. Relax and I'll be right out."

Sunday sits down and takes a few sips from her drink. Feeling tired, she quickly falls off to sleep. Avery shakes her awake. "I had to take a nap. I feel a little sleepy. I don't want to drink too much wine...that little bit that I drank made me feel so drowsy."

Unbeknownst to Sunday, Avery had slipped a date rape pill in her drink. "Go into the bedroom and get some rest," he says. "I'll see you in the morning."

"Okay, that sounds great. Goodnight Avery. I'm sorry I'm tired."

"It's okay, honey, go rest. I'll check on you later."

Later that night, Avery goes into the bedroom and finds Sunday asleep. "Hey baby, I want to lay near you. It's a little cold in there and the fireplace went down. The heat is on in here." Taking off his clothes, Avery gets into the bed and begins to fondle Sunday. He starts kissing her. She responds but is out of it from the pill.

Finally, she comes around when she feels his advances. She cries out to him, "No Avery, no! I don't want to have sex with you. Why are you doing this? Stop now...please."

He forces himself on her and breaks her virginity. Summer sits up on the bed in tears. "Why did you drug me, Avery? You raped me. I said no to you. Please take me back home."

"Sunday, you wanted it just as much as I did," he says sarcastically. "Stop acting like a kid. You're eighteen years old."

"I told you no. I wanted to wait until I was ready. Not here. I can't believe you tricked me to come here by telling lies."

"What? Wait on marriage? That's a long time to wait...think about all those years it will take for you to finish school."

Sunday cleans herself up, packs her bag, takes her car keys and begins to walk toward her car.

"Oh, so you are going to leave me here," Avery says. "Didn't you enjoy it like I did?"

"Hell no, I didn't enjoy being raped. My parents will have you locked up for this."

"You can't prove that I raped you. You volunteered to come with me and you didn't tell your Christian parents – and you agreed to register in my name. I can prove that much. Listen, I love you, and I needed to feel your body next to mine. I'm a man."

"You are a dog, Avery. You don't know what love is. You do all the things that love doesn't."

She gets in her car and leaves Avery at the resort. Avery calls her and begs her to come back and get him. They ride home silently.

"You're home, Avery. Don't ever call me again. I mean it."

"But what about our relationship?"

"We don't have one, you animal."

Sunday goes home. Walking inside, she calls, "Mom! Dad! I'm home."

"Sunday, you got back early," Clarice says, surprised. "We were expecting you in two days."

"The retreat was cut short because they are expecting snow. I'm tired…I'm going to head to bed."

"Oh, you went up in the mountains?"

"Yes, mom."

"Okay, well I'm glad you got back before the snow came, honey. Goodnight. We are turning in soon, too. We have a busy day tomorrow at church for the women's luncheon. Will you attend since you are back early?"

"No, I have other plans. Goodnight."

CHAPTER 13

A God of Another Chance

In the two months following her weekend with Avery, Sunday has been very distant from her parents, staying in her room all day and keeping silent about the rape. Clarice has begun to worry and Clark has been asking questions about how she is feeling.

Clarice calls to her, "Sunday, what are you doing honey? Will you be eating dinner? It's ready!"

"No, I'm not hungry. Eat without me."

"Okay, I'll talk to you after dinner."

"Okay, mom. I have stomach pains."

Knowing something is troubling her daughter, Clarice goes to her room and knocks at the door. "Are you okay, honey? You seem so sad for some reason."

"Mom, I'm okay. I'm just a little tired from preparing to leave for college."

"Your phone is ringing. It says Avery's calling."

"I don't have anything to say to him."

"Sunday, I'll be downstairs making a cake for church Sunday. If you need to talk to me, I'm available."

July has come and Sunday is excited about leaving her hometown and heading to Massachusetts to start at Harvard. Excited about her future, she hasn't yet realized that she has missed her period.

When she arrives at Harvard, the first person she runs into is Denzel. "Hi Miss Summer! Fancy meeting you here."

"How are you, Denzel?"

"I'm great, but I left my phone at a resort I visited…and your number was in it," he says, laughing.

"I understand," says Sunday.

"How about dinner this evening? Are you available?"

"Sure. I'm in building 7. Here's my new number. Call me and I'll come out."

"Okay! See you around 6ish?"

"Sounds good," Sunday says, feeling tired. She can't forget that terrible night in May with Avery.

Later, Denzel calls. Sunday goes outside to meet him and they head to dinner.

"What a beautiful restaurant," Sunday says. "Listen, I thought you were dating that girl in your math class – Sasha. What happened to her?

"No, we were just friends. She was a little too fast for me. I'm a man that likes to take it slow. I'm 23 years old and I am waiting on marriage before I touch a woman. It seems hard to believe, but it's true. I remember you saying the same thing when we dated. But then you met Avery and I lost touch with you. I thought for a minute that we were a couple for life. And I knew I had to wait until you were older, but I didn't mind."

"Denzel, are you still waiting?"

"Yes. And I feel that it's worth the wait."

"Denzel, I have a horrible story to tell you. Will you listen?"

"Sure. Are you okay, Sunday?"

"A couple months ago, I was invited to go to a retreat with my boyfriend Avery. He had other plans – more than just a retreat. We went to the resort, and when we got there, we attended a seminar on 'Relationship Building.' Afterward, we went to the cabin."

Looking bewildered, Denzel says, "You stayed in the room with him, Sunday? That is a no-no. I would have never done that. I would have gotten separate rooms. Keep talking."

"To make a long story short, he drugged my wine and then he raped me when I wasn't alert. I quit him and I haven't seen him since. If you don't want to talk to me anymore, I understand."

"Sunday, he should have been arrested for that. Did you tell your parents?"

"No. I was too afraid that they would take my car and that I wouldn't be able to come to college. I don't know, Denzel. I know I have to tell them one day, but it keeps haunting me – and I'm afraid of what they will think of me. I broke my promise to God and to them that I would wait until marriage. I'm baffled and afraid of what's going on within me."

"If you tell them, they will love you even more – just like I do. Sunday, I wanted to ask you to marry me after you finish college, but after you flipped over Avery, I gave up on you. And listen, I don't hold you accountable. I hold him accountable. He was a snake to drug your drink. And what do you mean 'within you?' What's going on?"

"Denzel, I think I'm pregnant."

"You must tell your parents. It is only fair."

"But I just started college. But since I started, I've been feeling sick and throwing up."

"Have you seen a doctor yet? You really need to see one so you can be sure."

"I'm sure I missed my monthly, and I feel like someone else is inside of me. Do I have to drop out of school?"

"If I were you, I would speak to my counselor and get advice. If you have to go home until the baby is born, then you can always come back. I'll be here waiting. I'm not giving up on us yet. Unless you still want to be with Avery."

Summer begins to cry. "I called Avery and told him that I think I'm pregnant. He said to abort the baby and said that he is not ready for marriage. And the girl I caught him with, Angie, just gave birth four months ago. Avery is going to Texas to be with her and his son. I am all alone in this, Denzel. What am I supposed to do?"

"Sunday do not abort your child. Do nothing but what I told you to do. Let me get you back home so you can rest and think. I'm here for you. Please don't abort your beautiful baby. God will provide for you. I know He will. My mom had me out of wedlock – and look how I turned out! Keep the baby," he says, hugging her.

After speaking with her counselor, Sunday decides to return home to tell her parents the news.

"Sunday, what are you doing home after two months in school?" Clarice asks as Sunday opens the door to her parents' home. "I thought your next break was at Thanksgiving."

Head hung; Sunday tells her parents the news. "Avery asked me to abort my baby, but I'm not. I know God will make a way and that I will return to Harvard."

After several minutes of silence, Clark says, "Honey, I know that things happen and that it is not your fault. We will stand by you. Keep my grandchild. Your mom and I are willing to keep the baby until you finish college."

Sunday begins to cry and hug her parents.

Months later, Sunday gives birth to a baby girl who she names Miracle Elizabeth Summer. She is so beautiful. Avery was asked to give up all parental rights to the baby since he didn't want to keep it anyway, and he sent a court paper to that effect.

Summer hears a knock at the door. "Mom, will you get the door? I'm feeding baby Miracle."

Clarice answers the door and is surprised to see Denzel.

146

"Sunday, I came by to see how you and Miracle Elizabeth are doing."

Surprised, Sunday says, "I didn't know you were coming. When I spoke with you last week, you said you were going home for the summer."

"No, I came to see my favorite girl. Where is Mr. Summer?"

Clark walks in the living room. "Hey Denzel. How are you doing, man? I haven't seen you since...I don't know when. I remember you said that you wanted to date Sunday when she got older."

"Yes sir, I sure did. Actually, I would like to ask you and Mrs. Summer if I could have Sunday's hand in marriage."

"Son, our answer is yes. We accept your wishes," Clark says.

147

"Sunday," Denzel says as he gets on his knees and pulls out a large diamond, "Will you marry me and let me be a father to baby Miracle Elizabeth? While we've been in touch throughout your pregnancy, I've been talking to God. He told me you are my soul mate."

"Yes, Denzel, I will marry you. All this time, God had my blessing, but I was looking in the wrong direction. God is a God of another chance. I didn't know He loved me so much."

Sunday and Denzel get married and settle in Massachusetts. Sunday goes back to Harvard, graduates, and becomes a pediatrician. As the years go by, she and Denzel have two more children. She never heard from Avery again.

ABOUT THE AUTHOR

Anne Gaynelle Johnson was born in Richmond, Virginia on May 9th. She is a licensed Evangelist at the St. Samuel Cathedral Church of God in Christ for 34 years, under the leadership of Superintendent Amos F. Kemper, III. She has been a song writer and play writer since 1980. She is a mother of three; Cleveland, Linda and Hope, 10 grandchildren, and 4 great-grandchildren.

I love you girls to life,

Evangelist Anne

Sunday Summer
Someone to Love Me...